All a Cat Can Be

Poems and Photographs for
New Start Cat Rescue

Together, we can make a difference

All a Cat Can Be
Poems and Photographs for New Start Cat Rescue

ISBN 978-1-9998004-0-6

First Published June 2018 by Eithon Bridge Publications
http://www.eithonbridge.com
email: eithonbridge@gmail.com

Copies of this anthology may be ordered from:
New Start Cat Rescue, Huntley, GL19 3EA
website: http://www.newstartcatrescue.org.uk
email: newstartcatrescue.org.uk

Cover photograph: Catherine Bradder

Printed by Stroudprint, Lightpill, Stroud, GL5 3NL

Introduction

New Start Cat Rescue is a not-for-profit charity run solely by volunteers, relying on fundraising and supporters to stay afloat. Our main aims are to rehome abandoned and unwanted cats and kittens. We also run a neuter and spay programme, and are proud of our links with our local communities. In 2017 we rehomed 750 cats and kittens. Sadly, this number will continue to rise with the number of owners and breeders failing to care responsibly for their cats.

This anthology is the creation of Sharon Larkin and Sheila Macintyre, friends from another time and life, who kept in touch on social media. Somehow, between word games and general chitchat, the idea of the anthology arose, like a sleepy kitten from its mother's milk. With Sharon at the helm the idea quickly grew and she corralled an amazing group of poets to create what has turned out to be a moving collection of cat poems. The response was overwhelming and the standard of poems high, making selecting a difficult task. So many poets love cats! Who knew? Sheila asked NSCR volunteers to provide photos, and worked with Sharon to pull the anthology together.

Thanks to Jackie Bahooshy, the charity coordinator, without whom the NSCR would be very different; to Sharon for her ability to herd cat people (not dissimilar to herding cats); to our photographers, and our patrons. A big *Thank You* to our volunteers, our supporters and everyone who contributes in some way to NSCR. Lastly, thanks to you dear reader, for helping raise funds. Together, we really can make a difference.

New Start Cat Rescue

Contents

Foreword

Are you supposed to have favourites when it comes to cats? I certainly do. I have three – Mousefur, Firefur and Peanut Butter. They are all rescue cats in Bangkok. Mousefur and Firefur were born in a local vets where someone had paid for their mum, a local street cat, to have her kittens. We took them in and they have been perfect house cats. We adopted Peanut Butter a few months later. She was a real street cat; she lived outside our apartment block where she gave birth to several litters over the years. Unfortunately someone kept putting poison out and most of her kittens died and we took her in as we worried that she was also at risk. She was filthy and pretty mangy, so we put her on a balcony and gave her food and water. Over the course of several days she cleaned herself up and put on weight and now she's a lovely cat. My daughter Sam named her because her calico colouring reminded her of peanut butter! She's very affectionate and whenever I sit on the sofa to work she sits next to me (my cat, not my daughter). She sometimes asks to go out but she only walks around for a few minutes before asking to come back in. She gives me head butts and soft bites when she wants my attention, and often sleeps next to me on the bed. I have always felt an affinity with street cats which is why I was so pleased to be asked to be a patron of New Start!

Stephen Leather, Author
http://www.stephenleather.com

Many years ago, I interviewed a young, good-looking, tall, blond guy for a job. He ticked all the job application boxes – and all of mine too! It was probably the least professional job interview ever. And by the time I'd discovered that he was single, we'd moved on to likes, dislikes and hobbies; '… and I do cat rescue,' he said. Wow! I smiled happily 'So do I…' He got the job, I became his boss, and eleven months later we were married. We moved into our home together, along with his rescues: Jack, Vinny and Lucy, and mine: Frankie, Claudia, Tootsie, Allie, Jemima and

Boris. After a bit of posturing and territorial hissing they all cosied down together – and our 9-cat family was born. But of course it didn't end there. Before long, having registered our brood with the local vet, he rang and told us about a large black cat who had been thrown out of a car on the A34... she had severe injuries, but would survive – and were we prepared to nurse her through her convalescence...? We were, and did, and of course she stayed. Rudy joined the family, swiftly followed by Dennis and Gavin, rescued from a locked garage after the owners had left. Both were boys we were assured, hence the names, but of course they were both pregnant females. Gavin and Dennis managed to produce eight kittens between them – Jonah, Dominic, Sebastian, Thomas, Clyde, Maddie, Emily and Moz. Oh, they were so sweet but we knew we'd have to find homes for them. 'Sadly they all have heart defects,' the vet told us when we took them for their first check-ups. 'You won't be able to rehome them... they'll have very short lives....' Little lives they may be, we thought as we took them home, but we'd make sure they were happy ones. They were. All eight of them lived happily with us until they were 18+. Then there was Lennox and Otis. And the ferals: Gus and Carlo, Luca and Flo. Not forgetting Alexia and Miranda, all injured, terrified, hurt, ill, unhomeable, all rescued via Cats' Protection, the local vets or word-of-mouth. Our massive rescued cat family seemed natural to us – not so much to others. Visitors looked slightly askance at cats draped happily over every surface, at the mountains of cat food boxes and dishes, at the huge fluffy welcome they got whether they wanted it or not. And going away took weeks of planning. We never went far, never for very long, and our very-carefully-chosen cat-sitters had reams of lists of likes and dislikes, medications and emergency phone numbers. So, that was how it all started... and now, as we come up to our silver wedding anniversary, we have Dexter and Dylan, and Daisy, David and Diego, and Danny, Desmond, Spotty Dotty and Skippy. Cat rescue is a way of life for us – and long may it continue.

Christina Jones, Author
http://www.christinajones.co.uk

Unusual Cats, Unusual Places

They said "This box will be nice for you"
from *The Cat from Katmandu* by Roger Turner
Photo, Rachel Slatter

Feral cats being fed in The Azores
Photos, Catherine Bradder

Alison Brackenbury
The Ladies, Paddington

But did you see it, where all day
the waters gushed, brass bolts tore nails,
mild grumbles that 'we have to pay'

died as the last step turned, so that
before attendants, knitting, sinks,
throned on its shelf, you saw the cat?

He always slept. His snoring filled
a basket for a middling dog.
Tawny and black, his stretched stripes spilled.

Pinned up above his glossy bulk
were his press cuttings: what he weighed
(more than a stone) how he would walk

dawn's platforms, just before the trains.
There was a cup, discreetly marked
'For the Cat's Food.' You paid again.

But once, he crossed suburban miles
to wastes of rugs, Saharan lawns.
He hated it, came back to tiles.

I have abandoned Brunel's lines,
steer case from coach (Victoria)
past pigeons' patter, neon signs.

Do you see, padding steps once more,
that cat I know you never saw?

Angela Topping
Savoy Hotel Cat

I am the cat, the ebony cat,
I'm neat and smart, though I don't wear a hat.
I grace your table, chic and serene
when the number of guests is unlucky thirteen.

The Savoy Hotel knows a black cat's best
to be a superior dinner guest.
I relish my smoked salmon and cream
when the number of guests is unlucky thirteen.

I wear a napkin round my throat
to help preserve my glossy coat
for it doesn't quite do to be less than clean
when the number of guests is unlucky thirteen.

The ordinary kitchen cats show me respect
for it's known my manners are fully correct –
my impeccable behaviour's a treat to be seen
when the number of guests is unlucky thirteen.

I've entertained the aristocrats in my prime,
heard many a fine tale on the old grapevine.
I've even graced the table of The Queen
when the number of guests is unlucky thirteen.

These human creatures are a puzzle all right
it seems it spoils their appetite –
they can't enjoy this fine cuisine
when the number of guests is unlucky thirteen.

Brenda Read-Brown
Chairman Mao's Cat

It must have been so difficult for you,
being the Chinese Chairman's playful pet.
When visitors said "Mao", you never knew
who they were calling. They would all forget
that depending on the tone, "Mao" can mean fur,
or cat. And your identity was gone.
Should you leave in disdain, or should you purr?
How could you understand what should be done?

But still, you went your individual way,
not like the rest, who wore a uniform –
re-educated, drilled, told what to say,
to think, to feel; taught how to perform.
A Mao, a mouser, you knew about rats,
and no-one ever managed to herd cats.

Mandy Macdonald
Because of the Cats

Back there, back then, on Sunday afternoons,
or more often after school, fewer people out hiking,
we walked, my two friends and I,
down through the grey-green bush
the perfumed haze of eucalyptus,
the silver breath of the silver trees
in the heat, singing

Alle-psallite-cum-luya – the cry of praise interrupted
by that breathless exhortation to sing it like a psalm
we sang in three parts as we went,
brown barelegged girls, drunk on strange music,
in procession along the crown-of-thorns path

In that heady, murderous landscape, every plant
wounds you: don't be fooled
by the delicately curled white fingers
of the silky hakea, the massed golden powder-puffs
of the kangaroo thorn;
they are all as spiny as porcupines
and the whole bush could burst into flame at any moment

But it never did
because of the two ginger cats who always walked with us

Roger Turner
The Cat from Katmandu

The sarcastic cat from Katmandu
  sailed off on a catamaran.
His friends all said "It'll be nice for you –
  on the Isles of Amber Zan."
  In fact they made it extremely plain
they didn't expect to see him again.

"You may be witty, you may be wise,
  but we don't admire your jokes –
they're far too clever. Please realise
  we're plain, straight-forward folks."
So they tied him tight to the catamaran
and sent him off to Amber Zan.

The men on the Amber Zan islands
  were round and jolly and fat
and they couldn't stand the cynical smiles
  and smart remarks of the cat.
So they said "This box will be nice for you"
and they shipped him off to Timbuctoo.
  So watch your tongue –
it could happen to you!

Julian Isaacs
Pussyfoot

Pussy smiled while the willow wept
  over a wasted land.
Washed lobster walls glinted pink
  tracked by trellis and net head debris.
Sniffing tyranny in Tehran,
  he yawned and kept on, calm.
His stretched blue tail uncurled in the Sanskrit sun
  shining in a Persian sky –
    they called him Shine
      though he never answered.
Sand sung its own song,
    while true grit blew a whiff of talc and Turkish delight
  on the invisible storm.
A murmur of purr smacked
  a whisker of sardine.
Languidly he licked the Nepenthean molasses
  at the white poppy's core.
The King and I were on in Siam
  but he remained a prince among porpoises.
By nightfall, once the sky held no shelter
  and the sun hid its swelter behind a rock,
    he would have caravanished,
    leaving only an imprint of French fern
      in the powder-dry dust.

Waifs and Strays

She descends as furtively as dusk from the poem *Stray* by Claire Thelwell
Photo, *Pixie* by Christine Cross

Cain-marked with a yin-yang, Phantom of the Opera face
from *Seconds* by Melanie Branton   Photo, *Two Face* by Christine Cross

Foster kittens – photo, Christine Cross

He incy-wincy-spidered his way up the curtains from *Seconds* by Melanie Branton
Photo, Catherine Bradder

Catherine Bradder
The Key

All that I can be is in your hands.

I could stay living in a barn,
I could live hiding away and die early.
We didn't ask to be born this way,
to live this way, to hide away, this way.

My purr to you, is in me, locked inside me.
Look into my eyes and see me.
You have the key to all I can be.
Please help us.

Emma Lee
Welcoming Honey

You couldn't tell us what you'd witnessed
when your previous owner fled to a refuge
and you came to us, chasing a screwed paper ball.
An outdoor cat, you charmed neighbours,
hated it when my husband shouted you off
his vegetable patch but on winter evenings,
you'd curl in his armchair, nudging him to lift
his book so you could pool furred warmth on his lap.
You dash behind the sofa at raised voices
and won't let anyone touch your stomach.
But, over the years, your purr drowns out
the fridge's hum, settling the household
into the rhythm of a relaxed heart.

Belinda Rimmer
Cuckoo

A cat has given birth
beneath a bush
to two black-spotted kittens,
both shivering in the spring sun.
Why not a barn?
Why here, on this hill,
at the mercy of dogs, foxes, cruel humans?
I observe from a distance;
far enough to be safe,
near enough to see a hint
of disinterest in her eyes.
She's young, barely a cat, and feral.
I tell her: *you need to suckle your kits.*
I like to think she'll stay
but a flickering doubt
says these aren't her kittens.

Claire Thelwell
Stray

She slides away, her origins
tangible only in a bolt of rust
across her chest like folded rock.
She descends as furtively as dusk;

lurks on tidy lawns, ignores
grasping hands and the mock rodent's call
from yellow doorways and suburban lanes
until she finds this pictureless hall,

this man, who does not scold, or summon
like fathers-of-brides, ringing champagne flutes
who call for silence so that they may fill it;
a man who stands, remote

and cool as caves.
They curl together, like bright roots
in the dark earth.

Melanie Branton
Seconds

He was my little killer whale
runtish, mewling dwindler of the litter
Cain-marked with a yin-yang, Phantom of the Opera face
bent banana, chocolate misshape
that failed to tickle the fancy of consumer choice.
My parents took him to spare him the ducking bucket,
a BOGOF with his more marketable, symmetrical brother.

But it was the roguish, stowaway pirate we came to love
as he incy-wincy-spidered his way up the curtains,
Jack-in-the-Boxed beside us on the side of the bath
or strutted around the house on pipecleaner legs too small for him.
His lifewish was a motor running inside him
a feisty shadow-boxer punching above his weight
an Evel Knievel daredevil flaunting wheelies in the face of fortune
and the leukaemia that blanked out his anaemic twin
snubbed him as surely as the consensus-shepherded pet pickers.
He was as bold as the slash pattern stained across his muzzle.
My parents thought that they had saved him,
but he undrowned himself.

Angi Holden
Temporary Home

The teenage girl proffers the cardboard box,
like a belated Christmas gift, her eyes appealing.
"Can you look after her please? Just for a few days?"
The words tumble out. "I found her in a puddle."
She frowns. "Only Mum says Arthur will eat her."
I conjure an image of Arthur, half a ton of furious
and spitting furball, territorial Alpha-Tom.
She's right. He wouldn't even spit the bones out.
"I'll find a home for her. Tomorrow. This week."
I'm doubtful, but agree, thinking of those tiny bones.
Two days pass, two weeks, two months. A year.
We have a daughter, move house, add a son,
another daughter. My childbearing years,
half my married life. Eighteen beautiful years
before I part company with my temporary cat,
before I settle Rags beneath the golden maple,
forever in her sun-washed patch of garden.

Jayne Stanton
My Cat is Sad

because the late September sun she tracks
across the duvet's hollow fibre tundra
marks a downturn into winter weight.

The moon lies drowning
in her water bowl; stars she can't unpin
refuse to sparkle on her bigger coat.

She's lost her sweeter side;
that paintbrush tail runs ever-widening circles
round her whiskers' under-estimation

and last month's escape routes hold her back
a little longer with each foiled attempt
to slip a tightening collar.

She doesn't know she's lost herself:
the changeling in a slanted past,
the stranger in tomorrow's photographs.

Cosseted Cats, Besotted Owners

All that I can be is in your hands from T*he Key* by Catherine Bradder

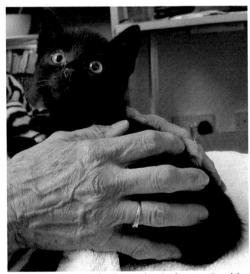

Both photos by Catherine Bradder

Content with stroking hands, from *Going Gently, Minnou* by Patrick B Osada
Photo, Catherine Bradder

Cosseted cats – Photo, Catherine Bradder

Angi Holden
Sunday Morning Cat

Back then, Sundays were for roast dinners,
newspapers, crumpets and cheese, both of us
relieved that the working week was done.
The car refuelled and washed, the cupboards
restocked on shopper-crammed Saturdays,
we turned off the alarm and waited for the thud
of newsprint and supplements landing on the mat.
While the kettle boiled, we'd let the cat out
watch her explore the borders, terrorise spiders.
In the lounge we'd share out sections: news, sport,
finance, motoring. Sheets spread across the floor
until the cat came in, picking her spot, rolling
onto her back, purring, belly exposed for a rub.

Josephine Dickinson
Miffy

At the black centres of your ochre eyes
is a lank-haired body needing caresses.
Your raw sienna burnt umber face
smoulders in the cupboard under the stairs.
They've hidden Esa's food which you prefer
to your dry chaff. You curl in a corner
at the top of the stairs, stretch, linger
as fingers stalk softly, low slung as a tiger,
sit in silence, slink in and out of your
own dark place. What do you think?
You prefer it here. Adoring hands.
Peep as they pad up the stairs.
Delicately as if you were a piece
of valuable china. Royal status.
You have the absence of other cats.
Solitude. Carolyn and Tim's bedroom.
They pick you up delicately.
You prefer it here.

Paul Brookes
A Cat Day

Long-haired big and black
Pilchard lounges on a rug
he thinks we bought for him.

Short-haired ginger and small
Jaffa relaxes on shabby chic garden chair
she knows we bought for her.

Jude Cowan Montague
A Night with Our Cat

He knows something we don't,
he really does,
and that's why he creeps between us,
tapping into what's underneath,
sensing what's not spoken but cried like a silent song,
directed by his orchid pinnae, he catches,
intricately performs our thoughts on his hammer and anvil.

We are not quite taking a breather
but we are on edge
and like rabbit glue he is stitching,
to tiny breaths, using his sleeping claws,
our distinct angles into one viewing point
where we look at the day from sleep's perspective,
wild and woody.

In the counterhills
he grows into a smooth grey god,
the lines on his fur absorbing our wrinkles.
The trichotomy moves with a rhythm that cannot be generated
by a faulty dyad. He gives back our animal psyche,
our dynamic, the good vibes
we were missing last thing at night.

Misty treetops. The sun rises.
Nurtured by his mini-rumble
echoed by the night-train that speeds to London,
we were transported as we dreamed
to wake into an alter-suburb
of beauty, goodness and truth,
we three transcendentals.

Jessica Mookherjee
Power Animal

Not quite alive, the cat is breathing a dream.
Small, mottled markings on his nose and paws
are black holes into which, eyes closed,
he takes in life force.
Each hair, down, glowing vibrissa

twitching to the background noise
of birdsong. Unstirred and unbroken.
I watch his guard-hairs bristle and one eye
opens to the sound of something
I can't hear.

Once, long ago, his kitten spirit flew
into my dream and as a small, ginger child
he slept by my feet,
in that spirit world.

There was a time before animals,
he told me, when there were only people.
Cat, bird and other peoples
that your ears and tongue
can't understand.

I watch him now with my mammal eyes
and whisper – stay with me a little while longer,
old man, and he breathes,
his mammal eyes shut,
he twitches and pounces in his sleep.

Chloë *of The Midnight Storytellers*
How to Annoy Poets

A proper poet must not speak of cats
You must not write about the rounded softness of fur
Smelling of summer fields and mouse blood

Don't witter on about campaigning for feline affection
Unless your listener has six months of quiet habits
A nose that is patient with cat pee
And a contract with a kindly fishmonger
Never write about purring
How the pitch and tone
Comfort cat and human hurts, and mend bone

No, the poet who wants respect
Can never confess
That when life wasn't worth living
The prickle of 12-week-old claws
Those tufts of fur between pink bean pads
Lifted the ancient weight from your heart
And made you giggle

Don't try to explain how
That breathing bundle of fur steadily shredding your collar
Was like cuddling a small, warm cloud
And someone said, Hope it doesn't rain
Never mention green alien eyes gazing straight into yours
Blinking with love
Or the trust given to you
To sleep carefully around your small companion all night

Oh no, never write about cats
Because proper poets will shut their hearts
And despise you for being sentimental. Meow.

Instinctive Behaviour

Pouncing cats, eyes bright with kittens prancing
from *Cats Pouncing* by Patrick B Osada. Photo, *Yoga Kitten* by Christine Cross

"There are no mice in this house" from *James Grey* by Avril Staple
Photo, *Shades of Grey* by Christine Cross

A feisty shadow-boxer punching above his weight
from *Seconds* by Melanie Branton Photo, *Kitten Fight* by Christine Cross

A fiery comet that burns itself out in an eyeblink from *Ginger* by Melanie Branton
Photo, *Gingy* by Christine Cross

Carrie Etter
Instinct

Everywhere they push
their claws in and hope
to find friction, to have to
tear them out

so I find the waxy
brittle husks on the teal rug
at the foot of
the leather armchair and

rising I unbend and sense
muscle and bone
sinews and ligaments—
I listen

for what's coming.

Nina Lewis
From Four Toes to Five

Our cat used to collect gifts of love,
not mice or frogs
just socks.
Laundry pile mountain
picked by easy claw,
cotton mouthed
he would find us
and deposit his love on the floor.

Avril Staple
James Grey

"There are no mice in this house", says James Grey,
pink tongue grooming flat his velvet fur.
Curled in his director's chair he'll stay,
practising a low, contented purr.

Outside a minty breeze conjures swirls,
throws tarantella seeds as winter bites.
Creatures gather nuts like precious pearls.
He watches from the corner of his eye.

Inside the house is safe, his work is done.
Nothing stirs, so he deserves this rest.
There are no mice tonight, except the one
he placed beside his best-friend's sleeping head.

Gareth Writer-Davies
Cat Logic

last night
the rats returned and sharpened their teeth upon the rafters

waking and woken
I picture them engaged in sapper duty

mining the felt
laying their babies in a long planned campaign of *lebensraum*

victory is a matter of numbers
soon

they shall gather
like a fearsome horde upon the soft borders

gnaw through the cavity walls
like panzers

the cat enters
with a rat in her mouth, stares at me

like I am a sook
with too much imagination and an insouciant need for domination

Patrick B Osada
Cats Pouncing

Pouncing cats, eyes bright, with kittens prancing.
Mocha hazy kittens love these
jinking and slinking cats, tails twitching.
Breeze, fuchsia scented, blows wind whispering
grass, shady over creeping
cats stalking kittens.

Kittens, stalking cats,
creeping over shady grass.
Whispering wind, blows scented fuchsia breeze.
Twitching tails, cats slinking and jinking.
These love kittens, hazy mocha,
prancing kittens with bright eyes; cats pouncing.

Carly Etherington
Spike

Yellow eyes
wide suns of Sahara,
stare at an empty bowl.

'Aarch'
The addict's miaow.

'Aarch'
From the open mouth
of the black and white boy,.
who has just finished his dinner.
Longing for his next meal.

Alison Brackenbury
Spotted

There is a glitter on the fence
Caught in my headlights' beam,
On hilltops in the stormy dark.
The town is lost, unseen,

But not this single star. An owl?
It is too sharp for deer.
It is the hunter, not the prey.
My breath grows quick, like fear,

But now I drive more slowly
Safe in my ton of steel
To catch it in the frozen glare
The hungry eye's next meal.

It does not lift on brindled wings
Or slither like a rat.
It turns a white disdainful face.
It is the hunting cat,

The latest in a careless line
Who haunt the sheds and barns,
Curl on old coats, in dusty sun –
Dogs are more dear on farms.

The rough dogs are shut up for night.
The farmer snores nearby.
The cat springs lightly from his mud.
She settles in the sky.

Lesley Quayle
Of Fish and Cats

We didn't have a cat but, if we had,
it wouldn't have been given
salmon, taramasalata or sardines,
but expected to work for its keep,
scourge of 'cow'rin tim'rous beasties,'
in to thieve our porridge oats and flour.

Your cat was Oriental, citrus-eyed and slender,
slinking over tartan cushions, linen laps, best porcelain,
a laconic, enigmatic shadow-cat, a waft-tailed,
pat-paw, snatch-claw spoil of lavish chum.

You came to stay in our three-a-bed, one-on-the-floor,
one-downstairs-on-the-couch scheme-end,
a strange and shining fish, jewel bright in our thin waters.
We sobered the family carnival, damped it down
like Sunday-go-to-meeting hair, rolled out a feast,
pale, golden curls of butter for the crusty bread
fresh from the oven, (Gran's face maroon, best apron floury),
thick sliced ham, boiled eggs, tomatoes, fish paste.

You loved the fish paste, effusive, said your cat would too,
more than salmon flakes or taramasalata or sardines.

Whatever the Weather

Like cuddling a small, warm cloud from *How to Annoy Poets*
by Chloë *of the Midnight Storytellers.*   Photo, Rachel Slatter

*My cat is sad because the late September sun she tracks across
the duvet's hollow fibre tundra marks a downturn into winter weight*
from *My Cat is Sad* by Jayne Stanton.   Photo, Rachel Slatter

White as pigeon's wing ... tall as sphinx in swift late winds of summer
from *Hot Spell* by Alison Brackenbury.   Photo, Catherine Bradder

She's a purr drifting on sunlight from *Junipurr Woods*
by Chloë *of the Midnight Storytellers*.   Photo, Rachel Slatter

Melanie Branton
Ginger

A scoop of apricot ripple
left to soften by the fire,
burnished chrysanthemum puff,
honey veined with dark amber,
wood-grained, watermark-whorled.

A hinge flips and at once
he's a conga eel
a floundering comma
a hammock of muscle and fur,
rockabye baby on the hearth rug,
his stomach rigid with cartilage,
a collapsible column of rings.

More moments bring more metamorphoses.
He delights like the balloon man at a children's party.
Sphinx - parcel - shrimp - kidney - croquet hoop.
When he walks, he seems to pour himself,
a fluttering taffeta ribbon, courtly favour,
or else he harums past, a fiery comet
that burns itself out in an eyeblink.

One minute you're dandling
a matelot-jerseyed urchin, the next
he springs like the jaws of a man-trap.

Cutesy-kitsch coffee-table figurine
ripped from an idol house.
Deceptively domestic,
its hard, slant eyes still demand
sacrifice of blood.

Alison Brackenbury
The Old Cat

How furiously you clean your white paws,
Soaked by the storm, in the kitchen's glow,
Which will soon be still at the garden's end
In the new moon's wash, the quiet of the snow.

Alison Brackenbury
Hot Spell

If my cats who once loved sun were here,
I would have Moth, the only tortoiseshell,
her fearless heart, her one black paw, small ears,
as webs flashed, deep sky burned the last of summer.

If my cats who best loved sun were here,
I would have Honey, white as pigeon's wing,
who never leapt to kill a living thing,
sit tall as sphinx in swift late winds of summer.

In high blue heat of this unseasoned summer
red Thomas, soot-black Bumble, striped Fizz run,
white-throated Moon steps from the dark of leaves
now all my cats are here who love the sun.

Jayne Stanton
A Kenning for Kitty

paw dangler
fish pond angler

bird stalker
tightrope walker

fine diner
mouse diviner

fur licker
city slicker

vase breaker
mischief maker

caterwauler
back yard brawler

bed warmer
nessun dorma!

Emma Lee
Make it Stop

A white paw pushed the blind aside
in the small hours so green eyes
could watch the fall of white flakes.
In her youth, she would have bounded
outside, sniffed paw prints and caught
flakes on her tongue until they melted
into cold wet and she'd turn inside,
whinge at the changed world.
Now, she sits on the sill, watching,
tail twitching a Morse: dot dash dash dot,
a plea to make it stop, out of time
with the drift of snow settling into a trap.

Phil Knight
Cool Cat Haiku

Ice cold winter day
there's fresh paw prints in the snow.
Cat seeks hot tin roof.

Cathy Bryant
The Cat Comes *after Sandburg*

The cat comes
on little fog feet.

It sits staring
into my face at 5 am
and motors its haunches
until I am thoroughly awake
and must feed it
before it moves on to a day
replete with important sleep.

Alice Ross
Cat in the Fog

Coalesced pad-prints on pavement dew
Lead to where the cat stalks
On his own and dustbin's business.
Twice furred, his own and the fog's,
Like the mist he banks, thins and disperses.
His nose lid-rubbed, his ears perforated
For love, grey like the fog
He twines along an irresistible aroma
To kipper-heads, chicken bones
And long-dead haddock.

Cats – and a Dog or Two

His snoring filled a basket for a middling dog from *The Ladies, Paddington* by Alison Brackenbury.   Photo, Catherine Bradder

His feline affection, her dog love from *Incompetible* by Sharon Larkin
Photo, Catherine Bradder

A basket for bread is now a basket for hairs from *Catterel as opposed to doggerel* by Mavis Moog.   Photo, *Heidi, by* Christine Cross

You have interests that are in conflict and opposite to mine from *The Cat Lover* by Jessica Mookherjee.   Photo, Catherine Bradder

Ann Drysdale
Old Cat Asleep

Mim dozes wheezily on the windowsill,
tongue a protruding tube, discoloured teeth
pinning her muzzle into a fixed picture
of sour disapproval.
A column of cold drool connects her scowl
to her uneasy feet, which grope and grip,
wielding unnecessary needles.

Unloveliness is overlooked; I love her.
Love? Love: I have known her a long time;
brought her from house to house, a living link
with all that muddled past.
She has put up with times of little care,
amused herself with the production of
a few indifferent kittens.

Apparently peripheral, although
she has affected several decisions
as resident responsibility,
part of the flow one goes with; who can tell
how great has been her influence?

She fritters hours, eyes closed, pulling and pricking;
unpicking petit point,
industriously kneading the idea of bread,
busy feet treading the slow mills of God,
squeezing small grapes of wrath.

Katherine Waudby
Survivor on a Raft of Curls

The kitten latched onto the poodle's curls.
He sucked and kneaded at the patient hound,
who looked up at us to see
if this was entirely necessary.

He looked like a furry cod fillet;
his pale stripes like the ridges in fish,
like the wrinkles on shorelines.
Splayed on the cream curls of our poodle,
he seemed so brave.
This tiny scrap
clutching his life-raft,
and trusting us all to love him.

Jessica Mookherjee
The Cat Lover

How do I love when I have no word for love?
Though I want to be beside you all the time,
I've become accustomed to your presence
that calms me and my anxious feral mind.
I see the easy life you give me but I could leave
if it wasn't to my taste and I complain
about the lack of meat at my table and the too

infrequent games. I cry and call at your
indifference when you have interests
that are in conflict and opposite to mine,
and that doesn't take away my feelings of
wanting to be with you all the time.
I think there is no feline word for love
but I feel your kindness when I turn my back.

Sharon Larkin
Incompetible

Why they'd arranged to meet, wasn't clear.
Something about shared interests, perhaps,
speaking in a familiar accent, having lived
in the same place for a spell, a fascination
for the wacky politics of a distant continent,
being fanatical about the same sports team.
But this big difference would break them
before they could take it further, and maybe
that was for the best. They began to stress
their lack of affinity to each other: his feline
affection, her dog love. Soon they'd drifted
back to their respective pets and settees
as if nothing had ever happened because
it hadn't. Cat dander always made her cry.

Mavis Moog
Catterel *as opposed to doggerel*

I offered him a pleasure dome of velvet and plastic
but my cat prefers the wicker bread basket.
It's not hygienic but see if he cares.
A basket for bread is now basket for hairs.

I offered him a golden bowl of chicken and cod fish
but my cat prefers to lick from the butter dish.
It's not hygienic until butter is hid
under a heavy, immovable, porcelain lid.

I offered him a loving home of playtimes and cuddles
and my cat loves to nuzzle and snuggle.
It's not hygienic but see if I care.
I'll bear all his germs for the moments we share.

Sandra Kemp
Cattitude

I'm a cat with panache, Rupert's my name,
I turn all the heads as I stroll down the lane.
I'm larger than most, with a size nine paw
and as soon as she's fed me, I'm off out the door.

My coat's black and white – the best one by far,
one ear's a bit bent but my tail's without par,
it curls with a flourish, my back's long and sleek.
There's no other cat like me, I'm simply unique.

When I've strutted my stuff I soon make my way
to a neighbour who loves me and likes me to stay.
She fusses and feeds me when I saunter in,
the dishes keep coming, I'll never be thin.

Now, fully loved-up and overly fed,
I slink up the stairs for a snooze on the bed,
worn out by her toys and tired of her smiles
but after this nap, I'll be out on the tiles.

Maggie Doyle
The Demise of Kevin the Cat

Kevin the cat lived in Fyffe
And had done so for most of his life
He lived by the shore
Catching fish by the score
Which he ate with a fork and a knife

On Sundays his favourite wish
Was to sit by the loch and just fish
He tickled the trout
Then pulled them straight out
Fried trout was his favourite dish

With his bucket filled to the brim
Thought he'd go for a dip, on a whim
Jumped into the loch
Spluttered and coughed
He'd forgotten that cats can't swim

Saying Goodbye

When I picked you up, you yielded loose–limbed in my arms
from *The Naming of This Cat* by Sarah J Bryson.   Photo by Rachel Slatter

Pale and delicate as a patch of snowdrops from *Bridge 19 Grand Union Canal,*
by Miki Byrne.   Photo, *NSCR Princess* by Christine Cross

Chloë *of The Midnight Storytellers*
Junipurr Woods

She is
A sneeze of fur on the breeze
Stripes of light and trees
She's a purr drifting on sunlight
Grass in summer soft as paws
Brambles on the ankle sharp as claws

Where she lies is overgrown
Lost and safe
These are her woods now

She lives
In the quiver of bluebells nudged aside
In double rainbows ten miles wide

She is
Scampering and drowsing, buzzing and burrowing
Singing and soaring
She is every sweet clear breath of air
Up there

My old cat lies buried in the woods
And we're both glad this is so.

Phil Knight
Ginger Cat

If you were to ask me what
I remember best about my childhood,
I would tell you about Ginger Cat.
The first time I saw him, he was so
                small
he was popped in my Mom's
                pinny pocket.
But that Cat grew and grew
to be The Toughest Cat in the World,
well on my side of Cimla Hill anyway.
Summer vacations lasted forever.
It was just him and me
holding back the hordes of Carthage
or Darth Vader's Imperial Fleet.

We passed from childhood
to teen together,
but those short animal lives
                are so cruel.
Each year he would lap me
seven times
on that fast inside track.
When I became a man
he was ancient,
the rich fur was brittle
        and grey,
but he was always there
after school, after college,
after work and
then he was gone.

Jennie Osborne
Dusty

You put your head in my hand,
scented stillness.
We shared deep conversation
of silent touch
exchanged the rough trust
of heartbeats.

When breath ran out,
when time stopped playing
in the long grasses,
I cradled you to earth
under a tree of butterflies,
left you salt water,
sad-coloured stone.

Miki Byrne
Bridge 19 *Grand Union Canal*

On the towpath
lay a small white cat,
curled as if asleep.
Pale and delicate
as a patch of snowdrops
nestled in dew-dipped grass.
Buried that day at Bridge 19
on the *Grand Union*,
with flowers planted
to mark her resting place.

Sarah J Bryson
The Naming of This Cat

Zelda, wife of F Scott Fitzgerald,
or character from a computer game?
Who cares? That was your name –
decided by family committee

in December 2011. You, my extra,
unexpected birthday present,
were softness personified
in tortoiseshell and white,

your stockings, fine whiskers
and bibbed front, all so pristine
from assiduous cleaning. You found
curled comfort in warm laps

or just by being near, stretched out
alongside your busy human.
When I picked you up, you yielded
loose–limbed in my arms; I cradled

you like a baby, your belly exposed,
as you gazed with those clear eyes
adoringly into my face. The shock of today
rings in my head, as I replay the scene again

and again – you with your life softness gone,
carried sombrely into the garden,
covered in a small blanket of respect
placed there by a passer-by, unknown.

Sarah J Bryson
The Morning After

The morning after April Fools' Day, I bury the ginger cat
wrapped in an old beach towel three feet down
in soft earth, under the *Viburnum plicatum* 'Mariesii'.

He's so stiff and so I have to dig the shape of the curve
of his back into the hole, so he fits in comfortably
as if 'comfortable' is a thing that still matters.

I push back the damp soil, press it down with gloved knuckles
and place a Cotswold stone slab over the site, scatter
some bark chip around, so it looks as if it's always been there

as I wonder if another cat may come, sometime
and lie in the shade of the tiered branches in May
or June under their white, lace-cap flowers.

Rachael Clyne
Jasper

I open a can of tuna, hear thump of paws
above – and leap from bed, rush
downstairs, eager for the tin
you plunge your whole face into
push around until lick-clean. It sticks
to your magnet key, legs splay
struggling to walk, till I pluck it from you.

The house – now clean of you. Heow
we meow-sang our mutual adoration,
mimicking your range of tone and chirrup,
diminuendoed into silent mouthing. Heow
you continually sought permission
to settle at my side, even though,
moments before, you did the same.

I remember your young hare-race body,
the sleek of you in your hunting days,
those fur-or-feathered corpses, so hard
to take. The only time you spoke human,
you fixed me with your gaze, *I'm dying*
clear as a knell in my head as we accepted
the hard lump that would finish you.

Patrick B Osada
Going Gently *Minnou*

Rescued from abuse – we had to build your trust –
you sat and watched our other cat and learned.
So timid then, your instinct was to hide
and once, in terror, threw yourself down stairs.

We watched and saw your confidence return –
the garden and the sun became your friends
and every day you'd make your way outside
or watched from windowsill on days of rain.

We gave kindness, food, shelter and a home
and in return you offered so much joy,
repaying us with closeness and your purr
and with a gentle love, so unreserved.

Now, as the days grow long, your life grew short
as age and illness wasted you away;
despite our care, the medicines and love
are useless now and can't postpone this day.

You rested, feather-light in midday sun
on friendly lap, content with stroking hands ...
and with a gentle breath you slipped away
like thistledown on wind ... and pain was gone.

Brenda Read-Brown
Flippy

Fur fell in my house. A selective snow
That covered cushions, people, throws;
A fine brown down, the moultings of a duckling
Unhardened yet by winter.

But this was far from baby fluff.
Flippy, old, but still as soft as stuff
That dreams are made on, gave us
Insulation with good grace,
Shedding drifts around the place
As if she didn't care
About her hair.

The furniture is cleaner now;
Clothes are bald again,
Defurred. I remember when
I met her thistledown with a curse.
But Flippy's absence is much worse.

Alison Brackenbury
Losing count

I am fifty, and the cat across my feet
Is seventy-five at least, but no one told
Him. So he yells, and gallops across paths,
Fights, and scrabbles cupboards till I scold.
We sleep our century in the ticking sun.
Here we shall stay, until the light grows cold.

Poet Biographies

Alison Brackenbury was born in Lincolnshire from a long line of shepherds and farmworkers. She won a scholarship to study English at Oxford, received an Eric Gregory award and a Cholmondeley award for her poetry and has published nine collections with Carcanet, the latest being *Skies* (2016). Her most recent book *Aunt Margaret's Pudding*, poems, recipes and memoir based on the life of her grandmother, is published by Happenstance (2018). Alison, now retired from the family business, lives in Gloucestershire.

Catherine Bradder is a Volunteer at New Start Cat Rescue and also fosters cats which she likens to mending something that's broken, or unlocking a door with a key. Catherine says that if it wasn't for the help the cats receive, they would not experience the relationship – being loved. And neither would the humans.

Melanie Branton's first collection, *My Cloth-Eared Heart*, was published in 2017 by Oversteps and her second is due to be published in late 2018 by Burning Eye. She is the pet human of an enormous fifteen-year-old ginger rescue cat called Adam.

Paul Brookes lives in a house whose owners are three cats. All named by his granddaughters, massive black long-haired Pilchard is the epitome of the phrase 'Scaredy Cat', Jaffa the lioness-like female is the Queen, lithe tigress-marked Bella, the youngest, was abandoned by her previous owner and lived four months as wild. She challenges the Queen.

Cathy Bryant's family cat was Chico, who brought Cathy up from age 2 - 22. From 23 - 40, Cathy was looked after by Wittgenstein, an adventurer tabby. Now Cathy's care needs are provided by Sacha and Sylvester, who rule with purrs. Cathy has also "written books and stuff."

Sarah J Bryson has owned many cats: the one in *The Morning After* was the third ginger, called Kenny after a cyclist. The one in *The Naming of This Cat* was a beauty, with black eye-liner and a feisty nature. Both were sadly killed on the main road. Sarah's poetry has been placed in competitions and published in anthologies, journals and on-line.

Miki Byrne has had three collections published and lots of individual poems in magazines/anthologies. The cat in her poem Bridge 19 was one of two that lived on her narrowboat years ago. Both were complete characters, would swim and were affectionate yet adventurous. Pippin tabby and Pandy are sorely missed.

Chloë *of The Midnight Storytellers* – A spoken word artist for some 20 years, enchanting family audiences and pioneering Story Cabaret. For over 30 years the feline pairs of Jasmine and Junipurr, Millie and Ella the Claw, and now Midnight and Mohinga have been Chloë's true family – in all their purring, claw-wielding, independent, fur-shedding, winter-night-warming comfort.

Jude Cowan Montague worked for Reuters Television Archive for ten years. She produces 'The News Agents' on Resonance 104.4 FM. Her most recent book is *The Originals* (Hesterglock Press, 2017). She lives in Mottingham with two grey cats, father and son, Lloyd and George.

Rachael Clyne describes Jasper as "bestest of all my cat-friends". Ever since reading Jungle Book, she wanted her Bagheera. Jasper's presence and amazing communication graced her life for eighteen years. Rachael's poetry appears in many journals and her collection *Singing at the Bone Tree* is published by Indigo Dreams.

Josephine Dickinson has been a lover and keeper of cats ever since Harmony and Melody graced her childhood. Currently, she is honoured to share her living space with Waldo and May, both rescued as kittens from the river by a kind shepherd friend. Miffy in her poem lived with her hosts the year Josephine was a reader at Wells-next-the-Sea Poetry Festival.

Maggie Doyle says her first cat "thought he was from Egyptian heritage, cherished by gods and their sons" ... until they named him 'Boots'! Meanwhile, Maggie says *she* enjoys the titles of 'Worcestershire Poet Laureate Emeritus', 'Miss' in school workshops and, best of all, 'Nanny'. Her poems have been published in anthologies.

Ann Drysdale has always had cats ever since Buster arrived on her ninth birthday. They have formed a furry thread that has run through her life ever since. Trevor, Mortimer, Molesworth, Pootle, Tynwald, Tom and Mim have all left pawmarks on her heart. Ann now lives in South Wales with Asbo. Her poetry collections include *The Turn of the Cucumber*, *Gay Science*, *Backwork*, *Between Dryden and Duffy*, and *Quaintness and Other Offences*.

Carly Etherington and her partner are known as 'the cat couple'. Their cat, Elizabeth, goes by many names, a favourite being 'Our Dear Old Queen'. Spike, the inspiration for her poem in this book, is a cat that Carly cat-sits. Carly paints and writes about cats – see her website www.carlyetherington.co.uk

Carrie Etter – Growing up in Normal, Illinois, Carrie Etter's house had 6-14 cats at any one time, depending on litters of kittens. Presently she lives in Bath with her husband and two rescue cats, Susu (short for susuwatari) and Max. Her fourth collection, *The Weather in Normal*, will be published by Seren Books in November.

Angi Holden was adopted by an abandoned kitten. Rags shared her family home for the next eighteen years, surviving the onslaught of three children. Much loved, she was irreplaceable – just as well since Angi has developed a severe fur allergy, and is sadly unable to have another cat.

Julian Isaacs aka Auntie Pus *(The Punk Balladeer)* has been writing and performing poetry for nearly half a century, and first sold his poetry in pamphlet form in the corridors of Kensington Market in 1971. A lifelong Gene Vincent fan, he knows you can never tame a wild cat.

Sandra Kemp has always enjoyed writing in some form or other, especially occasional poems. Cats have always been part of her life. From playmate in childhood to companion in older age, some cats have been adopted by Sandra, others have adopted her.

Phil Knight from Neath, has been published in *Poetry Wales, South, Earthlove, Planet, Dail 174* and others. In 2015 *Red Poets* published his collection *You Are Welcome To Wales*. *Ginger Cat* was his beloved childhood companion and the first of his many cats. The last (for now), Suki, passed in 2007.

Sharon Larkin isn't sure how she came to be involved in the anthology project but her enthusiastic co-editor had a lot to do with it! Sharon's poems have been widely published in anthologies, magazines and on-line. She has a pamphlet forthcoming from Indigo Dreams Publishing. https://sharonlarkinjones.com

Emma Lee's most recent collection is *Ghosts in the Desert* (Indigo Dreams Publishing, 2015). She co-edited *Over Land, Over Sea: poems for those seeking refuge* (Five Leaves, 2015). Emma reviews for The High Window Journal, The Journal, London Grip and Sabotage Reviews and blogs at http://emmalee1.wordpress.com

Nina Lewis is the current Worcestershire Poet Laureate, published in anthologies, magazines and online. Her début pamphlet, *Fragile Houses,* was published by V. Press in 2016. She is a cat-lover and was lucky enough to own a rescue cat. She recently won a Haiku Slam with cat poems.

Mandy Macdonald is a cat-loving poet who hasn't had a cat of her own for twenty years. Cats have adopted her throughout her life, however, since the day two sibling cats walked out of the Australian bush and occupied her garden when she was fourteen; her poem *Because of the Cats* is based on a true story of her schooldays in New South Wales. She plans to keep cats again if she ever actually retires.

Mavis Moog's current cat is a three-year-old son of a rescue-cat. Nimby likes to sleep in the bread basket, go on camping holidays and make big fur mountains with his 3 doggy siblings, when they all snuggle together.

Jessica Mookherjee is published widely and was highly commended for best single poem in the Forward Prize, 2017. Her inspiration for the poems in this book – dearly loved ginger friend of 18 years, Clarence – passed away on 29 December 2017. Clarence was a Battersea Dogs Home cat, explaining his poetic outsider nature. She misses him.

Patrick B Osada is not sure which came first, a love of poetry or keeping cats – both have been a major influence on his life for almost as long as he can remember. Patrick explains that when submitting his poems for this book, Phoebe, one of a long line of rescue cats, was helping him to typesjgr mkugbf kj----- www.poetry-patrickosada.co.uk

Jennie Osborne has shared all her adult life with cats. One, Dusty, died tragically young. Two, Sheba and Purdy, who lived to a great age had dementia in their last months. Jennie has two poetry collections from Oversteps Books, *How to be Naked* and *Colouring Outside the Lines.*

Lesley Quayle is a widely published, prize-winning poet and a folk/blues singer. She's had cats all her married life, mainly moggies and farm kittens, and one pedigree Persian, inherited after her owner died. Elegant, aloof, this unexpected house guest never quite lived down the fact that her given name was Piggy.

Brenda Read-Brown can't imagine a home without a cat. Currently, she has Tippett, who likes to help her write. Despite this, Brenda has completed two collections (*Arbitrary edges*, 2013 and *Like love*, due later this year from V. Press). When Tippett allows her out, Brenda takes part in poetry slams; she has won 32.

Belinda Rimmer has had a varied career: psychiatric nurse, counsellor, lecturer and creative arts practitioner. Her poems have appeared in magazines, on-line and in anthologies. She has read at Cheltenham Literature Festival, and won an award to have one of her poems turned into a film. She has never owned a cat, but adopted one as a kitten, along with half of the neighbourhood. She named the cat, Wilma.

Alice Ross has, until recently, always had a family cat: Kitty, Moriarty (evil, with blue steel claws), Orlando (a marmalade, of course), Tinkle, Pusska and, dearest and sweetest of all, little timid Miaousi, an abandoned newborn stray she brought up from a few hours old.

Jayne Stanton is Head of Staff to her two cats, Archie (retired hunter, radiator hugger) and Bonnie (doorframe etcher, carpet shredder). She has written poetry commissions for a county museum, University of Leicester's Centre for New Writing, and a city residency. Her pamphlet, *Beyond the Tune*, was published by Soundswrite Press in 2014.

Avril Staple's poetry has appeared in many journals and poetry anthologies. James Grey – in contrast with the photograph on page 32 – is a Maine Coon who owns several families on the street. He doesn't write poetry.

Claire Thelwell lives in Cheltenham with her husband and two children. Her poem *Stray* was inspired by her grandfather who found a loving home for a stray cat he rescued, only to find her at his door two weeks later. She followed him everywhere for the rest of her life.

Angela Topping has never been owned by a cat, but fondly remembers her schoolfriend's cat Felix. She has admired cats from afar and they seem to creep into her poems from time to time. Her favourite pattern is tortoiseshell. Angela's Poetry has been widely published; her latest collection is *The Five Petals of Elderflower* (Red Squirrel Press).

Roger Turner is widely published in poetry magazines and anthologies. Formerly an architect and garden designer, he has also published five books on garden history, garden design and plants. He has two beautiful cats called Freddy and Zoë.

Katherine Waudby's current cat is a three-year-old son of a rescue cat. He lives with three dogs and a blind jackdaw in Derbyshire, but loves travelling. During the summer, the whole family take their caravan all around Britain.

Gareth Writer-Davies describes himself as a cat-sitter and future owner of a tortoiseshell cat. He has twice been shortlisted for the Bridport Prize and commended/highly commended in the Welsh Poetry Competition. He became Prole Laureate in 2017. His pamphlets *Bodies* and *Cry Baby* were published in 2015 and 2017 by Indigo Dreams Publishing.

Notes and Acknowledgements

Page 12 **Angela Topping – Savoy Hotel Cat**
The famous London hotel employed a cat who was brought to the table to make up numbers whenever thirteen people were sharing a table. The poem first appeared in *The New Generation,* Salt Publishing, 2010.

Page 24 **Jayne Stanton – My Cat is Sad** was published in her pamphlet, *Beyond the Tune*, by Soundswrite Press, 2014

Page 37 **Patrick B Osada – Cats Pouncing.** This palindromic poem appeared in Patrick's first full collection, *Close to the Edge.*

Page 38 **Alison Brackenbury – Spotted** was previously published in *Snakeskin.*

Page 44 **Jayne Stanton – A Kenning for Kitty** was previously published in *Poetry in the Waiting Room* (for Derby hospitals) vol 5, autumn 2009 and *Catlines* anthology, autumn 2010.

Page 49 **Ann Drysdale – Old Cat Asleep** was published in her collection *Between Dryden and Duffy* (Peterloo, 2005)

Page 52 **Sharon Larkin – Incompetible** was first published as *Pet Hate* in *Reach* magazine, Indigo Dreams Publishing, in March 2014

Page 58 **Phil Knight – Ginger Cat** was previously published in *Earthlove,* 2006

Page 63 **Patrick B Osada – Going Gently, *Minnou*** appeared on his website http://www.poetry-patrickosada.co.uk

Page 64 **Brenda Read-Brown – Flippy** was published in her collection *Arbitrary Edges* (2013)